Beautifully Broken

Giving God the Broken Pieces

———————

Mandy Fender

ISBN 978-0-9822190-2-7

Dedication

For every woman who has ever felt broken.

Psalm 107:14 "He brought them out of darkness, the utter darkness, and broke away their chains."

Isaiah 61:3 "...to give unto them beauty for ashes..."

Psalm 147:3 "He heals the brokenhearted..."

Ecclesiastes 3:11 "He has made everything beautiful in its time."

Acknowledgements

Thank you to my mom, Ramona, who taught me how to be a woman of God; Mom, thank you for all of those early mornings and late nights that you stayed up to pray for me. Thank you for helping me in the editing process of this book!

Thank you to my mom-in-law, Becky, who spent countless hours helping to edit and publish this book. Thank you for always helping me with all of the questions I had.

Last, but certainly not least, thank you to my husband and children. Brandon, you have always been an encourager to me and my dreams. I thank you for that! Tyler and Jadyn, thank you for being patient with me during the writing process. I love you all!

Table of Contents

Preface

In the years that I have served in youth ministry and in women's ministry, I realized a common thread that ran through us all. I saw young women and mature women seeking guidance, love, and forgiveness. I saw that we all wanted to feel beautiful but sometimes needed that extra encouragement to feel that way.

As I stood in the altar praying with women through the years, I asked them all the same question, "Did you know that you are loved?" Their beautiful tear-stained faces stared back at me with their heads shaking 'no.' I realized that far too often we walk through this life without truly knowing how beautiful we really are and without knowing how much we are really loved by God.

My prayer is that I encourage everyone who holds this book in their hands to know they are beautiful and they are loved!

Introduction

The word 'broken' is not generally paired with the word 'beautiful.' In this book you will find why being broken is indeed beautiful. To be beautifully broken is to be broken before the Lord. Being broken before the Lord allows Him to put you back together the way He sees fit. It allows God to put you on the potter's wheel and make you who you were always meant to be.

Jeremiah 18:4 "But the pot he was shaping from the clay was marred in his hands; so the potter formed it into another pot, shaping it as seemed best to him."

Sometimes what we think is best is actually not the best for us. God knows the beginning from the end and knows how to make you whole. Your brokenness is not the end of who you are; it is the beginning. Life will break you, but God will mend you and make you stronger through it all. The society in which we live approaches brokenness with trying to fix it themselves. We cannot fix ourselves. The truth is only God can turn a life that is broken into a thing of beauty.

We are surrounded by images of beauty and expectations of outward appearances. The world will inundate you with how you should look and act, but only the Word of God will show you who you really are and what you should really do. Each and every person has a specific purpose that God has designed just for them. Yes, God took the time to map out a plan for your life.

Jeremiah 29:11 "For I know the plans I have for you," declares the LORD, "plans to prosper you and not to harm you, plans to give you hope and a future."

The only way you will find that plan is to be broken before Him. A transformation must take place in your heart so that God can shape you and mold you into the vessel He has designed for His plan. God's plans are always better than ours!

Psalm 40:5 "Many, LORD my God, are the wonders you have done, the things you planned for us. None can compare with you…"

Being beautifully broken can at times seem difficult and seem like God is asking too much of you. If you could see to the end, you would see it is always worth it. There will be growing pains, but the pain means you are growing! It is time for the believer to be set apart. No more fitting in with society. We do not fit in because we are different. Our beauty comes from within, and we must learn the value of this.

The broken beautiful seem to have it all together on the outside, but on the inside, they are a mess and not a beautiful one. They feed their fleshly desires and give in to temptations while looking flawless on the outside. Their outward beauty is the only thing that defines them. If only they could know there is so much more. Outward beauty fades, but inner beauty will shine throughout your lifetime.

You can grow to the point in Christ where He can freely use everything in you, even what you call flawed. Let God use your broken past so He can transform it into a beautiful future. You are not the broken beautiful; you are the beautifully broken.

Beautifully Broken = Trading your ashes for His beauty

To trade your ashes and receive His beauty, you must be willing to surrender and be broken before the Lord. For example, take the seed. A seed has to be broken before it can produce. It must be broken in fertile ground for it to thrive. When the seed is in the proper environment and breaks, it begins to develop. Once the seed breaks and dies, growth begins.

This is how we should give our will back to God. We have to ask ourselves, "Are my ambitions God's ambitions for me?" Learning to die to yourself and surrendering your will is invaluable in your walk with the Lord. Just like the seed, once you break and die to self, your growth in the Lord begins.

Will this be a challenge? YES!

Will you want to give up sometimes? YES!

Everyone has their moments, but it is those who never give up and continually submit their brokenness to the Lord who prevail and produce good fruit.

Mark 8:35 "For whoever wants to save their life will lose it, but whoever loses their life for me and for the gospel will save it."

John 12:24 "Truly, truly, I say to you, unless a grain of wheat falls into the earth and dies, it remains alone; but if it dies, it bears much fruit."

2 Corinthians 4:16 "Therefore we do not lose heart. Though outwardly we are wasting away, yet inwardly we are being renewed day by day."

Outwardly, this life is like a vapor, but inwardly, God will renew you and make you strong.

The next part of this book will take you inside the Word of God to look at the places in your life where you might be broken and see how Jesus can make you whole. It will show you that God can make the broken places beautiful. Toward the end of each chapter, you will get to take a look inside the lives of beautifully broken women in the Bible and read their stories from their points of view.

Everyone has a story. What's yours?

Only you can decide which one you will be.

The Beautifully Broken or The Broken Beautiful

Chapter One

Beautifully Loved

Before you can know what love is, you must learn who love is. The world will try to tell you how love should look and how love should feel and will try to define what love is to you. But the world's view of love is broken; one minute it loves you and the next it doesn't. That's not the love anyone really wants, and that is not the love for which anyone should strive. Love is learned, so who will you allow to teach you what love really is?

From a very early age, you embrace what you think love is by what others tell you and show you that it is. The only problem with that is human love is flawed and not perfected. Often we have too many distorted takes on love because of the way everyone else represents it. That is why divorce rates are so high; the world view of love is absolutely broken. The word 'love' is thrown around carelessly and out of context which makes it hard to know what love really is.

The question, "What is love?" can be answered when we find *who* love is.

Who is love? God is love (1 John 4:8)

Know who God is and you will know what love is.

You do not have to settle for the world's love; there is a

greater love in store for you. The love of this world cannot compare to the love of your Savior. There is a perfect love that is just for you. Most women dream of a fairy tale love. Well, you already have it. You have a Man, who loved you more than His own life. You have a Man, who literally died so you could be with Him. Jesus is that Man. He loves you to infinity and beyond. Seriously, to infinity and beyond! His love really is for now and forever. He loves you with perfect love that heals the heart and mends the holes that life leaves behind.

You might have had your heart broken by someone. Maybe it was a friend who broke your heart or maybe a relationship that did not last, or someone did not live up to the promises they made you. Jesus takes those pieces that other people have broken and makes your heart whole again. His love fills the void that other people leave behind. His love is the only love that could ever truly make you whole. The love that comes from God will never leave you broken-hearted.

All anyone ever really needs is to be loved, I mean truly, deeply, and sincerely loved with a love that is defined in 1 Corinthians 13.

1 Corinthians 13:4-8 "Love is patient, love is kind. It does not envy, it does not boast, it is not proud. It does not dishonor others, it is not self-seeking, it is not easily angered, it keeps no record of wrongs. Love does not delight in evil but rejoices with the truth. It always protects, always trusts, always hopes, always perseveres. Love never fails. But where

**there are prophecies, they will cease; where there are
tongues, they will be stilled; where there is
knowledge, it will pass away."**

God is love! That means that God is all of these things to
you. He is patient with you, kind to you, does not
dishonor you and He is not easily angered with you.
When you ask for forgiveness, God does not keep a
record of your wrongs to hold against you later and
throw them in your face. God rejoices in truth and not
evil. He protects you and entrusts you with blessings. He
has hopes for you and His love perseveres for you. He
does not give up on you and fail you. He loves you; He
always has and always will. God knows the secrets of
your heart, the struggles of your past, and your every
thought and still loves you. His love truly endures.

When you have had your heart broken so many times, it
is hard to receive love when it is shown to you. You may
not know whose love you can rely on and trust. You may
have had questions about who loves you running through
your mind like:

Do they love me because of what I can give them? Do
they only love me because of what I can do for them? Is
this love real? Is it forever? How do I know they really
love me? How do I know I really love them? Can I trust
them with my heart? Will their love for me last?

There is one love that you never have to question, and
that love is from God. You do not have to question it. He
has already proven it by giving us Jesus as our Savior.
Never ever doubt the Father's love for you because:

Romans 5:8 "But God demonstrates his own love for us in this: While we were still sinners, Christ died for us."

That means while you were in the middle of your sin, God still loved you enough to send you a Savior, to send you a way to be free from sin, a refuge, a hope, a true love. When you turned your back on Him, He still loved you. When you cursed His name, He still loved you. When you sinned against Him, He still loved you. He loved you enough and still loves you enough to bring you out from among your sin and make you righteous through the blood of Jesus Christ.

His love has never been in question and should never be a question in your mind. Whether or not you receive that love and reciprocate that love is entirely, one hundred percent, up to you. How you respond to God's love determines the rest of your life. To receive His love, you must break down the barriers you set up against love and against God. Break the stereotypes of what love is, break away from what you thought love was and what the world told you love has to be.

Become broken in your flesh so that your spirit may receive the true love that was always meant to be in your life. His love will heal the ugly, bitter, painful brokenness and replace it with the beauty of real love. Let His love into every part of your life and every part of your life will feel love. If there is ever a moment you feel unloved or if in any way your heart has been wounded, remember your first love. All other loves will pale in comparison to His love. There is nothing that comes close to His love for you, not on this earth or in the universe or in any other universe for that matter.

Love is not fully realized until Jesus is in it, and it cannot reach its full potential without God.

Your search for the fairy tale love ends here; you do not have to search any further. His love is yours for the taking. Rest assured you are beautifully loved by the Maker of heaven and earth. Love is a choice, and you have to embrace the fact that you are indeed loved. Once you realize His love, you have to remain in the knowledge of the truth that you are loved by Him. Do not walk out on the love God has to give you for anyone or anything. You must convince your flesh of the facts and tell yourself beyond a shadow of a doubt that you are loved by God, the Father, and let nothing separate you from that fact.

Romans 8:38-39 "For I am convinced that neither death nor life, neither angels nor demons, neither the present nor the future, nor any powers, neither height nor depth, nor anything else in all creation, will be able to separate us from the love of God that is in Christ Jesus our Lord."

Leave no room for doubt in your mind about love. Go to the Word and remind yourself daily God is love and He loves you!

Now that you have received His love freely, go out and freely love. The Bible tells us to walk in love, do everything in love, to love your neighbor, and to even love your enemies. This is a whole lot easier to say than it is to do, but it is not impossible. You might have to stretch yourself quite a bit to live a life of love, but it will most definitely be worth it. Loving others with Christ-like love pleases God, and pleasing God brings blessing.

2 John 1:6 "And this is love: that we walk in obedience to his commands. As you have heard from the beginning, his command is that you walk in love."

1 Corinthians 16:14 "Do everything in love."

These scriptures tell you that love is not to be turned on and off. Love is an all-the-time thing in which you are to walk and with which you are to do everything.

What does this mean? It means to be patient and kind in everything, with everyone, and everywhere you go. It means do not be selfish and do not boast. It means to honor those around you. It means to forgive and trust God. It means never to lose hope in anything at any time. This is the challenge: to love at all times.

Galatians 5:14 "For the entire law is   fulfilled in keeping this one command: "Love your neighbor as yourself."

You can keep God's entire law by this one statement. How beautiful is that? Love will keep you from sinning against others and God. Love will keep you in truth.

Love will keep you patient and kind toward other people around you. Now, who is your neighbor? Anyone with whom you come in contact... the teller at the bank is your neighbor, your restaurant server is your neighbor, and your boss is your neighbor. Love your neighbors; it is a command.

This next verse will be the hardest one.

Luke 6:35 "But love your enemies, do good to them, and lend to them without expecting to get anything back. Then your reward will be great, and you will be children of the Most High..."

Is it even possible to love your enemies? Yes! You can love your enemies by praying for them and being patient with them. Even be kind to them. There is an old saying that says to 'kill them with kindness.' Showing love through kindness is a great weapon against enemies. It can actually even show your enemies the way to Christ over time. You can never go wrong when you obey the Word of God. When the Word says to do it, there is a reason for it and a reward in it, so love even the worst of your enemies.

Love has the power to change your life and the lives around you. Let His love overflow from you and the fruit of love in you will pour out to others. When we love like Christ, people will be drawn to Him because of the way His love makes everyone feel. Remember how His love makes you feel? Don't you want your family, friends, and neighbors to feel that too? There are so many people in the world who are the broken beautiful, meaning they might look okay on the outside but on the inside they are hurting, maybe even like you once were. Do not hold back the love of Christ; let it shine through you.

His love is the light that will bring salvation to the lost, hurting, hungry, and sick. Part of the fullness of His love is sharing it with others. So the next time you have the opportunity to share His love, just do it! His love can be shown through the giving of your time, a loving word, or a lending hand. This kind of love was never meant to be kept to oneself and boxed in. It has always been meant to spread like a wildfire once you receive it. His beautiful love is for everyone!

Learn about love from:

The story of Hosea and Gomer

Her Testimony…

My name is Gomer; I became the wife of a prophet of the Lord named Hosea. Imagine my surprise when this man of God wanted to become my husband. I was a promiscuous woman who had no real intentions of settling down. But how could I refuse such a proposal? I married this man, Hosea, and gave birth to his children.

He was a good husband to me and always treated me well, but my past ways got the best of me, and I slept with another man. To my amazement, Hosea searched for me and came back to get me even after I did this horrible act against him. He held me in his arms and showed me true love. I was shown a love like never before, a love that I was not sure I deserved. Hosea told me that I was to be faithful to him, and he would do the same for me. He said we were to be together.

The Lord uses my story to reveal to you the true power of love. A love so pure and forgiving that nothing in your past can hinder it or change it. It is a love that remains through pain, hardships, and mistakes. My marriage to Hosea was God's way of showing Israel His love for them. Hosea's complete love toward me represents God's complete love for you. I had to learn to be beautifully broken so that I could receive true love.

Her Breaking Point: Seeing True Love

Just like Gomer, our past sometimes gets the best of us and we make mistakes. Sometimes that can make us feel undeserving of God's love because His love is so pure and so perfect. We see ourselves as lowly and unforgivable and search for other loves to fill the void of the true love we think we do not deserve or have the right to expect.

The old saying, "You accept the love you think you deserve," rings true through the lives of many. God's love is not something that is earned; it is something that is given. So whether you think you deserve that love or not, receive it and embrace it because it is for you! Ask for forgiveness and the ability to overcome your past.

God is willing and faithful to help you through your past. It is important that you understand His love and the beauty He wants to trade you for your ashes. You must also learn to love yourself and learn from your mistakes, but do not let them destroy you and define you. You are not the mistakes you have made. You are God's beloved. You can be totally free from your past through Jesus Christ. His blood can wash away your sin and make you white as snow in the eyes of God.

The true love of God is found in 1 Corinthians 13. Remember, God is love, so that means He is all these things. Let His love conquer all.

God's love for you perseveres through all of your mistakes. He loves you so much that, even while you were still a sinner He sent Jesus to die for you. Never doubt the love God has for you. His love is true, real, and tangible. When Hosea wrapped Gomer in his arms, she could feel just how real love is. God is willing to wrap you in His love so that you can feel the warmth of His embrace.

To be beautifully broken is to accept the love God has for you.

You are beautifully loved! Tell yourself every day:

I AM BEAUTIFULLY LOVED!

Chapter Two

Beautifully Forgiven

Step one of forgiveness from God is realizing everyone needs forgiveness. You are not forgiven because you are perfect; you are forgiven because Jesus is perfect and He paid the price for everyone's forgiveness. All forgiveness requires of you is sincere repentance. There are dark places in everyone's heart that need forgiving. All you have to do for forgiveness from God is ask for it with a sincere heart. No matter how good you think you are, you still need Jesus to cover your sin. At the same time, no matter how messed up you think you are, the blood of Jesus IS greater than your mistakes, failures, and past.

1 John 1:8-10 "If we claim to be without sin, we deceive ourselves, and the truth is not in us. If we confess our sins, he is faithful and just and will forgive us our sins and purify us from all unrighteousness. If we claim we have not sinned, we make him out to be a liar and his word has no place in our lives."

Forgiveness comes only through Christ alone. Jesus is the key to our forgiveness.

His blood unlocks righteousness and covers your sin with it.

Matthew 26:28 "This is my blood of the covenant, which is poured out for many for the forgiveness of sins."

Psalm 32:1 "Blessed is the one whose transgressions are forgiven, whose sins are covered."

Sometimes you might feel like what you have done is unforgivable and that you have let everyone down, disappointing them and yourself. This brings about negative thoughts and sometimes even suicidal thoughts. Understand you are not alone. We have all sinned and fallen short of His glory (Romans 3:23). Do not tear yourself down when you sin. Pick yourself up, ask for forgiveness, and move forward working on doing better. Your past does not define who you are now and does not have to determine your future.

In the Bible, there is an account of a man named Saul who had to overcome his past. Saul was a well-educated man with a great disdain for Christians. He actually saw many Christians to their death. He was a murderer. You might know him today as Paul in the New Testament. Saul was converted to Paul when he had the revelation of who Jesus Christ really was. Every day he carried the weight of who he used to be and what he used to do. The only way he could carry on in this life was forgiveness. He had to let God forgive him, and he had to forgive himself, which meant giving all that weight of his past to Christ.

Philippians 3:13-14 "Brethren, I do not regard myself as having laid hold of it yet; but one thing I do: forgetting what lies behind and reaching forward to what lies ahead, I press on toward the goal for the prize of the upward call of God in Christ Jesus...."

Paul had to let go of the past. He had to forget those things he used to do and forget those words that used to describe him and look forward to his hope in Jesus Christ. Let the blood of Jesus cover your past. Let God be greater than who you used to be.

Was what Paul did terrible? Yes. Was God able to forgive him? YES! Was Paul able to become great in the Kingdom of God? YES!

God can still use you no matter what your past. You have to decide to look forward and not back. Your past is your testimony and not the final verdict.

Isaiah 43:18 "Forget the former things; do not dwell on the past."

Do not be held captive by past sins of which God is ready to forgive you. You have to let God forgive you and learn how to forgive yourself. Forgiving oneself might be one of the hardest things to do, but it is essential in the forgiveness process. God is able to remove those sins from your life as far as the east is from the west.

Psalm 103:12 "as far as the east is from the west, so far has he removed our transgressions from us."

Not only that but, when you are born again through Jesus Christ, you are literally a new creation. He is able to make you beautifully new. It's not about how messed up you think you are or were; it is about how good you know God is. You should never beat yourself up about who you used to be. Who are you now? If the perfect God of love can forgive you, then you can forgive yourself for who you used to be and for the things you have done.

2 Corinthians 5:17 "Therefore, if anyone is in Christ, the new creation has come: The old has gone, the new is here!"

Let the old you go, and put on the new you. You do not have to keep going back to the same things you used to do because they are not you anymore. Learn not to revert back to who you used to be just because it's easy. There has to be a new routine formed in your life once forgiveness is embraced.

2 Corinthians 4:1 "Therefore, since God in his mercy has given us this new way, we never give up."

There is a new way to live that God will show you when you read His Word. The new way of living may seem difficult at first but stick with it because you will soon see that living His way is indeed better than living the old way. Not only is it better, but it will also be much more rewarding to live life.

Live a forgiven life without taking forgiveness for granted. Do not keep picking up what Jesus finished on the cross. He took it to the cross so that you can be free from it. Jesus would have you to go and sin no more, but again, if you do sin, remember His mercy is fresh every morning.

Lamentations 3:22-23 "The faithful love of the LORD never ends! His mercies never cease. Great is his faithfulness; his mercies begin afresh each morning."

Through being beautifully forgiven you allow God not only to forgive you but you also allow Him to make you beautifully new. Sometimes you might just need to renew your newness. This means to remind yourself daily that you are, indeed, forgiven from everything and in all ways when you trust Christ for that forgiveness.

Jesus becomes your Hope and your Mediator. When God looks at you, He sees you through the covering of Christ which makes you white as snow.

Once you have embraced forgiveness from God and have forgiven yourself, it is time to forgive others.

The most important thing you can learn about forgiving others is that forgiving them is not about whether they deserve forgiveness from you or not. It is about doing for others what God has done for you. If God can forgive you then surely you can forgive the "them" in your life.

As they were crucifying Jesus, Jesus prayed a prayer for those who were killing Him. He prayed to the Lord for their forgiveness and said 'they do not know what they were doing' (Luke 23:34). If our goal in life is to strive to be like Christ, then our goal must also be to forgive no matter what. Jesus proved that forgiving, even what we think is unforgivable, can be done. He proved it on the cross when He prayed that prayer.

Every time you forgive you are giving the power back to Christ in your life. Forgiveness says I will trust the Lord to justify the situation, I trust the Lord to bring me peace, and I trust the Lord for my vindication. Have strength to forgive. It will not always be easy, but it will be worth it. It might hurt at first, but that forgiveness will allow your hurt to be healed. If you choose not to forgive, you have chosen to be disobedient to Christ and set up a barrier against God.

Matthew 6:15 "But if you do not forgive others their sins, your Father will not forgive your sins."

You see, when you do not forgive someone you might think that you are setting up a barrier against them, but in truth you have set up a barrier against yourself and your relationship with God, the Father. That is why it is so crucial that you forgive and forgive quickly, so you do not have those negative barriers in your life. Do not poison yourself with grudges and bitterness; trust God and forgive. Always remember forgiveness is about obedience to God and not whether or not the person has earned your forgiveness.

When someone does you wrong, take a deep breath and forgive as God has forgiven you.

Learn about forgiveness from:

The Woman Caught in the Act of Adultery

Her Testimony...

As they dragged me out of my house, I scrambled to find something with which to cover myself. I cannot believe that I was caught in my sin; now I will pay for it. Surely I will be put to death for what I have done.

They pulled me through town and threw me at the feet of a man named Jesus. I wept uncontrollably knowing what was soon to come. I heard them discussing my punishment and how the law said I must be stoned to death. Through my blurry gaze, I saw Jesus bend down and write in the dust of the ground. While my accusers still cried out for my punishment, Jesus stood up and said, "Let anyone of you who is without sin be the first to throw a stone at her."

He wrote on the ground one more time and then stood again and asked me, "Woman, where are they? Has no one condemned you?"

"No one, sir," I said.

"Then neither do I condemn you," Jesus declared. "Go now and leave your life of sin."

That moment changed my life forever. I should have been put to death, but instead, I received forgiveness. This man, Jesus, silenced my accusers and made me free. Now, I knew I must go and leave the sin that once controlled my life. I had to become beautifully broken so that I could be beautifully forgiven.

Her Breaking Point: Complete Forgiveness

Jesus' forgiveness is immediate and compassionate. A lot of times we do not realize how quickly and faithfully God forgives us. The blood of Jesus is greater than what you have done; you just have to ask for forgiveness. We, as women, are so hard on ourselves and each other. Why? We must learn to forgive ourselves and others. Her story shows us how we must leave the life of sin for a different kind of life.

God forgives, but that does not give us an excuse to go on sinning. Just like God told this woman, I believe He is telling us to leave our life of sin. We are to be new creatures in Christ and not revert back to who we used to be before we were at the feet of Jesus. But, if you find yourself thrown down in life, remember at whose feet you are. You are at the feet of Jesus. Just look up and receive your forgiveness.

You will always have accusers. There will always be someone trying to bring up who you used to be, but again, that does not define you. The Bible tells us that Satan is accusing us to the Father. Just because someone accuses you does not mean it's who you are. Remember who your Mediator is. Jesus, Himself, is your Mediator. When anyone accuses you of that for which you have been forgiven, Jesus dismisses it for you. When you are free in Him, you are free indeed even from your accusers.

Is there any dust that has settled in your heart?

Do you have accusers in your life?

Let Jesus write in the dust of your heart and let Him transform you from the inside out. Let Him silence your accusers. One of the hardest things to overcome in your walk with Jesus is overcoming who you used to be. Some have an easier time with this than others, but it is necessary for everyone to do.

You might always be remembered to some as the person who you used to be, but to God and other believers you are an entirely new person. They say people can't change themselves, but change can come from God. God can open up our eyes to see differently and our hearts to new beginnings. God gives us the power to change, the power to be different than we used to be, the power to overcome, and the power to see life in a whole new way.

To be beautifully broken is to be at the feet of Jesus, completely forgiven.

You are beautifully forgiven, and you can beautifully forgive others!

Every day, say to yourself:

I AM BEAUTIFULLY FORGIVEN!

Chapter Three

Beautifully Created

Have you ever wished you could change something about yourself? Most women would probably say a big loud "YES!" If you have ever felt like you were not enough, not smart enough, not strong enough, not pretty enough, not talented enough... this chapter is for you. You are enough because Jesus has given you more than enough to be who He has called you to be. Acknowledge who you are in Christ and let that be your reflection. Know that who you are in Christ is more important than who the world thinks you should be. Realize your beauty in Him. How you feel about yourself really changes your outlook on life. Self-confidence, self-worth, and acceptance of who you are can mean all the difference when it comes to what you accept and expect in your life.

If you feel badly about yourself then, generally speaking, you accept less for yourself. You see what the world calls beauty and get totally discouraged because you might not fit the mold for their beauty. But if we take a deeper look at the definition of beauty, not the world's definition but God's definition, we will see a whole new world.

When God sees you, He sees His creation and His creation is beautiful. Just like when we see the beauty of the sky and the beauty of the oceans, that is how God sees us. God does not make mistakes; do not let anyone tell you that you were a mistake because you are not a mistake! You are created by Almighty God, and He created you beautifully with love and a purpose.

Genesis 1:27 "So God created mankind in his own image, in the image of God he created them; male and female he created them."

To understand that you are beautiful, you have to believe this verse. God created us in His image to be like Him, and He is beautiful; therefore, you are beautiful. Do not let anyone tell you otherwise. You might not like everything about the way you look but who does? Wrap your mind around the fact that you were created in His image.

The world may not understand your beauty but that does not change the fact that you are beautiful. You are God's masterpiece.

Ephesians 2:10 "For we are his workmanship."

Who says you have to be a certain size to be beautiful?

Who says your hair has to be a certain way to be beautiful?

Who says you need makeup and certain types of clothes to be beautiful?

Who says we need to be airbrushed?

Answer: THE WORLD

Now,

Who says you are His masterpiece?

Who says you are fearfully and wonderfully made?

Who says you are created in His likeness?

Who says you are beautiful?

Answer: GOD

Beauty is in the eye of the beholder, so who will you allow to behold you?

Your beauty is not determined by the size of your waist or the color of your skin or the locks of your hair. Your beauty is on a whole other level; you are out of this world's league. You are in this world, but you are not of this world. Your beauty is based on the Word of God. You are defined not by the outside but by what is found on the inside. And if what is found on the inside is beautiful, it has a way of seeping through to the outside. You are probably thinking…Oh great. 'Another "you are pretty on the inside, and it's what's on the inside that counts" speech.' And you'd be right, but I believe what is on the inside can truly make the outside beautiful.

For example, if you have joy on the inside, and it shines through on the outside by a smile then you have learned how to let your beauty on the inside make you beautiful on the outside. So let what is on the inside of you shine through to where all people see is your joy, peace, hope, and love that Christ has put on the inside of you. That is what is truly beautiful and is a beauty that lasts. When you look in the mirror, let the reflection you see be based on how God sees you, not how man sees you. Let your reflection reflect Christ.

1 Peter 3:3-4 "Your beauty should not come from outward adornment, such as elaborate hairstyles and the wearing of gold jewelry or fine clothes. Rather, it should be that of your inner self, the unfading beauty of a gentle and quiet spirit, which is of great worth in God's sight."

People may be looking at your outward appearance, but not God. God is looking straight at your heart. There have been many people who have been absolutely beautiful on the outside but terribly ugly on the inside. Once their beauty faded, they were left with nothing. Beauty is temporary and can only make you temporarily happy. There are beautiful people who are broken and hurting because they lack the knowledge of what true beauty is. That is why the Word tells us not to concern ourselves with outward beauty and not to trust in beauty because one day it will be gone anyway and what will be left is found on the inside.

Proverbs 31:30 "Charm is deceptive, and beauty is fleeting; but a woman who fears the LORD is to be praised."

The answer to who you are will always be found in Christ. Your identity is in Him. Just refuse to let vanity be your identity. Refuse to let vanity dictate your life. It is time to get a new standard of beauty. Let's get a Godly standard of beauty where we view others not by what they wear or how they look but by their hearts.

Remember there may be someone who looks like they have it all together on the outside but on the inside, they may be torn and broken. No matter how beautiful someone is on the outside, they still have to deal with internal struggles of their own. If you could focus on how God sees beauty rather than how man sees beauty, you would surely be blessed and relieved of all the pressure of this world's standard of beauty and come to the conclusion that you are beautiful!

With the knowledge of true beauty comes confidence. This is a confidence that can't be taken away by the world because it was not given by the world. This confidence is not in ourselves but through Christ, who gives us the strength to be confident and courageous in all situations.

You were created to be strong, confident, and victorious through Jesus Christ and that is beautiful! You can be secure in yourself when you are secure in Christ.

Learn about being beautifully created from:

The Samaritan Woman

Her Testimony...

It started off as just an ordinary day in my life. I walked to the well to retrieve water as I did every day, but this day was different. This day I met a man named Jesus who changed my life forever. I began to draw my water from the well when He asked me to give Him a drink. It was to my surprise because I was a Samaritan and He was a Jew. We were of different lives and backgrounds. Who was I to interact with Him? He told me that if I truly knew who He was that I would be asking Him for a drink.

This confused me at first, but He continued talking and brought up things that He could have never known. He told me to call my husband and when I told Him I couldn't He revealed to me parts of my life that only God knew. This man, Jesus, was a prophet. Not only a prophet but the Messiah! He told me things and opened up my spiritual ears to hear the truth. He was, is, my Savior! Once I received the revelation of who this man was, and who I was in Him I could not keep it to myself. I went back to town and shared everything about Him that I knew. He revealed who He was to me and transformed my view and my way of thinking. I was changed when Jesus spoke to me. He will give the drink that will make you never thirst again!

Her Breaking Point: The revelation of who Jesus really was and who she really was in Him

Once you receive the truth of who Jesus is, and who you really are, it should change you forever. Just like the Samaritan Woman, you should share the good news of Jesus everywhere you go. When she received the revelation that the Messiah was here, she could not keep it to herself. I like to think it just bubbled out of her and God's goodness just overflowed from her heart because of the revelation she had received.

Have you ever been that excited about Christ?

Has God ever revealed anything to you that you couldn't keep to yourself?

Maybe you met Jesus in a similar circumstance. You may have not grown up in church. You may have had an entirely different upbringing but somehow, someway, God managed to meet you at the well of your life and talk with you. And you received the revelation of who Jesus truly is and who you really are. God is so good and will speak to the heart of every man and woman. They just have to listen. God might use you to be His voice just like He used the Samaritan woman's voice when she went back to town.

When the Samaritan woman went back to town, lives were changed because of her testimony of Jesus and what He had done in her life. She learned from her brokenness. God can use you in the exact same way. You have been through some things, and you have learned a lot along the way. Now you can share it.

Jesus said if she truly knew who He was, she would be

asking Him for a drink.

Sometimes we need to stop and remember who Jesus really is to us and who we truly are in Him and ask Him for a drink. That drink can represent anything in life, but we must ask. We must commune with God and meet Him at the well every day of our lives. You are a priceless, one-of-a-kind, mosaic masterpiece! God is taking all those little pieces that you do not like about yourself and shaping them in His hands to be beautiful.

To be beautifully broken is to know who He is and who you are in Him.

You are beautifully created!

Every morning as you look in the mirror to get ready for the day, tell yourself:

I AM BEAUTIFULLY CREATED!

Chapter Four

Beautifully Destined

Have you ever wondered what this life was all about or what your purpose was? Have you ever asked yourself: What are we here for? Does everyone have a purpose in this life? Does this life have any meaning?

Everyone who has been created has a purpose. You have a purpose in this life and your life absolutely does mean something. Before you were even born, God knew you and designed a plan for you.

Jeremiah 1:5 "Before I formed you in the womb I knew you, before you were born I set you apart; I appointed you as a prophet to the nations."

Jeremiah 29:11 "For I know the plans I have for you," declares the LORD, "plans to prosper you and not to harm you, plans to give you hope and a future."

God has big plans for you, but you have to decide whether or not you will follow those plans. If you follow His plans for your life, you will prosper, and you will have hope for a beautiful future. His plans will require you to stay on the straight and narrow path, so your path can't follow the crowds.

1 Peter 2:9 "But you are a chosen people, a royal priesthood, a holy nation, God's special possession, that you may declare the praises of him who called you out of darkness into his wonderful light."

You are chosen, and you have a purpose! You are to do good works which God will show you through His Word. As believers, we share the same purpose, which is to worship God, to serve Him first and foremost and to be the light unto this world.

You are meant to light up the room when you walk in. You are destined to dream dreams. You are destined to be successful. You are destined to be prosperous. You are destined to be ambitious. You are destined to be victorious.

Your destiny comes when you fulfill the purpose God sets for all believers. You will not just fall into your destiny; you are going to have to work for it. Work toward the goal by doing what the Word says.

The Word says your purpose is to worship and praise God. Your purpose is to be the light of the world. Your purpose is to pray and intercede. Your purpose is to serve. Your purpose is to give. Your purpose is to share the good news of Jesus Christ.

You also have a personal purpose that God gives you. You find your personal purpose while fulfilling your general purpose as a believer. God has a specific plan for your life. Stick to the plan. Once you do the things you were purposed to do as a believer, then God will reveal your personal purpose to you. God gets involved in the details of your life. He will be thorough when you are thoroughly seeking Him. He will give you the details of your personal purpose because He is a personal God.

God has given us all unique gifts that will be used in our personal purpose. All of our gifts and talents are different and must be given back to God to be a part of your purpose.

What are you good at? What are the gifts that God placed on the inside of you? Those gifts can be used for the purpose God has given you. If you can cook, then cook. If you can clean, then clean. If you can encourage, then encourage. If you can help, then help. If you can sing, then sing. If you can give, then give. If you can serve, then serve. There are so many things you can give back to God to fulfill your purpose. Do what you can where you are. Start fulfilling your purpose today by doing what you can to serve the Lord and others.

Romans 12:6-8 "We have different gifts, according to the grace given to each of us. If your gift is prophesying, then prophesy in accordance with your faith; if it is serving, then serve; if it is teaching, then teach; if it is to encourage, then give encouragement; if it is giving, then give generously; if it is to lead, do it diligently; if it is to show mercy, do it cheerfully."

1 Corinthians 12:4 "There are different kinds of gifts, but the same Spirit distributes them."

Everyone has gifts. Some of your gifts are hidden deep within you. If you seek God to see them, He will show them to you. Some gifts you have may seem small to you, but they are not small to God. Never diminish your gifts, but rather, appreciate them and let them grow in you. Whatever you do, do as unto the Lord and let Him lead you in the direction you should take with your gifts. The important thing about your gifts is that you give them back to God to show His glory. Let God use your gifts and talents, and in doing so, you are fulfilling part of your purpose. If you love God and are called according to His purpose, then it always goes back to His plan for your life.

Satisfaction in this life comes from fulfilling your God-given purpose. God will point you to your individual purpose when you listen with your spiritual ears. Fleshly ears can't comprehend Godly purpose. There will be people in your life who may not always understand your purpose and why you always point your life in the direction God gives you, but if you keep on pushing for God's purpose in your life, you will be rewarded. Fulfill your Biblical purpose and God will show you your personal purpose.

1 Corinthians 2:9 "But as it is written, "No eye has seen, no ear has heard, and no mind has imagined the things that God has prepared for those who love him."

God has prepared beautiful things for you in this life and the next. When you love God, you will love His purpose.

His purpose for your life will not always be easy and, in reality, it will probably always be a step of faith. Trust God with your future because He has already planned one for you. Allow Him to tell you your purpose because He has already seen it. He has prepared a purpose for you.

What you do with your life should always link up to the Word of God to see if it is in God's will for you. You were destined for so much more than this world has to offer; your life matters and your purpose matters. God can open doors for you of which you have not even thought. God has entrusted you with things to do. Will you do them?

You can begin to serve in your purpose no matter your age. Young or old, if you have breath in your lungs, you still have a purpose. Do not let anyone despise you because of your age. If God told you your purpose, then stick to it. It is important that you understand that purpose is not about comfort. You will have to step outside your comfort zone to fulfill your purpose sometimes. Step outside yourself and into the will of God.

If you are still unsure about what God's will is for your life, remember that His perfect will is always found in His Word.

If it is your purpose and you are in the will of God, then God will provide a way for it to come to pass. You work your faith, and God will work out a way.

Matthew 6:26 "Look at the birds of the air; they do not sow or reap or store away in barns, and yet your heavenly Father feeds them. Are you not much more valuable than they?"

How much more important are you to God than the birds of the air, and He still cares and provides for them. He will care and provide for you and help you in your purpose. God will make a way for you to fulfill your purpose. Provision for the purpose comes from God.

Matthew 10:30-31 "But the very hairs of your head are all numbered. "So do not fear; you are more valuable than many sparrows."

If God took the time to number the hairs on your head, then you better believe He will take the time to help you fulfill your purpose. You are important to God. What you do with your life is important to God. You are destined for greatness, destined to win, and destined to be more than a conqueror.

Ephesians 1:11 "In him we were also chosen, having been predestined according to the plan of him who works out everything in conformity with the purpose of his will."

Romans 8:28-30 "And we know that in all things God works for the good of those who love him, who have been called according to his purpose. For those God foreknew he also predestined to be conformed to the image of his Son, that he might be the firstborn among many brothers and sisters. And those he

predestined, he also called; those he called, he also justified; those he justified, he also glorified."

God has destined you for a great purpose. Work God's plan. God is faithful to those who are diligent in His plans. Let Him be the one to call, justify, and glorify your purpose. Your purpose is not truly fulfilled until you have fulfilled God's purpose.

Learn about purpose from:

Mary the Mother of Jesus

Her testimony...

An angel began to speak to me and told me things concerning my purpose. He told me I would bear a son. The idea that I would give birth to a son confounded me. I was so young, was not married, and had never even been with a man. How could this ever become my destiny to have a son who would be great in all the earth, a son who would reign over every kingdom? I was not even royalty.

The angel continued to tell me the words of the Lord and encouraged me with the fact that no words from God ever fail. I embraced the Word of God concerning my future and knew that His plan would be fulfilled in my life. I was God's servant, and I would listen to His perfect will for my life. Soon I was with child from the Holy Spirit and began to show the signs of pregnancy. I knew not everybody would understand or believe in my destiny, but to me, all that mattered was that I was fulfilling it whether or not they understood it. I trusted in the Lord to see me through, and He did. He revealed to my future husband, Joseph, that I was indeed carrying the son of God and that Jesus was a part of his purpose now too.

Together we would fulfill God's holy plan and together we would raise Jesus as the Lord instructed us. Because I fulfilled my purpose, I was blessed. I was blessed to see Jesus grow up. I was blessed to see Jesus work miracles, and I was blessed to see Jesus become the Savior of this world. I was blessed to be a part of the greatest story ever told.

Her breaking point: Letting go of what she thought her purpose should be and embracing God's purpose for her life

Mary probably had set out goals for her life and had her own plans, but she let them all go so that she could fulfill God's purpose for her life. She realized that first and foremost she was the servant of God. She placed her destiny in God's hands instead of keeping it in her own hands. She knew that what God had in store for her would always be greater than what she could do on her own. She had to let go of the idea that it was impossible. Remember that all things are possible with God. God has given you the ability to fulfill your purpose; you just have to say 'yes' to His plan. Everything you need has already been placed on the inside of you. Unlock your potential by allowing God to push the limits that you have placed on yourself. You are more capable than you know. Do not limit yourself by staying in your comfort zone.

The Lord qualifies you for your purpose, not man, so do not worry about what they are going to say. If you have ever struggled with what direction to take in your life, remember, the Lord will direct you. God will not force you into your destiny, but He will show it to you if you are willing to look and listen. God is looking for hearts that are open to Him and His will. Is your heart open to God's plan?

You can do this. You can fulfill your destiny. It is not impossible. Start to fulfill your purpose now, right where you are at. What's stopping you? Who will you let hold you back? Start now! Just do it! Begin to praise and thank God right where you are. Trust that His Word will come to pass in your life. He will keep His promises to you concerning your future. He will order your steps if you allow Him to. Do not take your life into your own hands when your life can be in the hands of God. Always let Him be the director of your destiny. Your life is worth living, and only YOU can live it!

Proverbs 16:25 "There is a way that seemeth right unto a man, but the end thereof are the ways of death."

God's ways are higher than our ways. His plans are better than ours so let Him determine your future.

To be beautifully broken is to surrender your plans into the hands of God.

You are beautifully destined!

Whenever you doubt your purpose, tell yourself:

I AM BEAUTIFULLY DESTINED.

Chapter Five

Beautifully Free

Have you ever wished to be free? Free from stereotypes. Free from people's opinions. Free from anxiety. Free from hurt. Free from fear. Free from guilt. Free from shame. Free from addictions. Free from the pressures of this life.

God has given us everything we need to be free today.

John 8:31-32 "Jesus said, "If you hold to my teaching, you are really my disciples. Then you will know the truth, and the truth will set you free."

To be free, you have to know the truth. What is the truth? The truth is the Word of God. To gain freedom in every area of your life, you have to know the truth about every area of your life. Find out what the Word says about your situation; believe what it says and you will be free. Sounds simple enough, but it takes faith on your part to receive it. Not only do you have to know the Word, but you also have to believe and trust what it says about you and your situation.

If you would like to be free from stereotypes, then you are going to have to shake off the chains that stereotypes have placed on you. Break free from what others say you have to be because of where you came from. You came from God first so be who He says you are. In order to break free, you need to know and believe what He says. You are more than what others say you are.

If you would like to be free from people's opinions, you have to break free from caring what people's opinions are. You have to learn to care more about what God says than what they say.

If you would like to be free from anxiety, you are going to have to go to the Word of God and find the truth. Give God the cares of this life. Give your negatives to God and He can make it a positive.

1 Peter 5:7 "Cast all your anxiety on him because he cares for you."

Psalm 138:8 "The LORD will perfect that which concerneth me."

Anxiety is an attack on your faith and an attack on the truth. The truth is you do not have to be anxious for anything; you just have to pray and believe God will take care of it. Anxiety robs you of the freedom Christ has given you. God is willing and able to perfect everything that concerns you. You just have to trust and believe that He will. Be free from your anxiety in Jesus name.

If you would like to be free from fear you will have to trust God to help you overcome that fear.

**Psalm 34:4 "I sought the LORD, and He answered
me; He freed me from all my fears."**

God wants to replace your fears with power, love, and a
sound mind.

**2 Timothy 1:7 "For God hath not given us the spirit
of fear; but of power, and of love, and of a sound
mind."**

Fear is not from God. Fear will make you retreat and
make mistakes. That is why God wants to free you from
all fears. No matter if your fears are small or great, you
can give them all to God, and He can give you the power
to overcome them.

If you would like to be free from guilt and shame, you
will have to go to the Word of God and believe what it
says about your guilt and shame. Jesus finished your
guilt and shame on the cross! Jesus is so awesome!!!

**Colossians 1:22 "But now He has reconciled you by
Christ's physical body through death to present you
holy in His sight, without blemish and free from
accusation."**

When you are in Jesus, you are holy in God's sight. You
are free from the accusations against you because Jesus
took what you were accused of upon Himself on the
cross. You are free from the blemishes in your life!

If you want to be free from addictions, that is possible
through Christ too! Addictions are things that have
become habitual in your life. Anything can become an

addiction if you let it. Addictions can be anything from food, to too much television, to drugs. You can be free from those addictions when you give them to Christ. Your addiction does not have to control you. When you give that addiction to Christ He will fill the spot that the addiction once filled. Cravings for that addiction can be broken when you hope and trust in the Lord and get into His Word.

1 Corinthians 10:13 "No temptation has overtaken you except what is common to mankind. And God is faithful; he will not let you be tempted beyond what you can bear. But when you are tempted, he will also provide a way out so that you can endure it."

There is a way out! Every day is another chance to be free. Focus on giving no place to the devil. Do not give in to the temptation of your addiction. Surrender to God and you won't surrender to your addiction.

1 Corinthians 7:22 "For the one who was a slave when called to faith in the Lord is the Lord's freed person; similarly, the one who was free when called is Christ's slave."

Become a slave to Christ and you won't be a slave to your sin. Whatever you do not master will master you so master your addiction by surrendering completely and fully to Christ. There will always be chains that try to bind you, but as long as you're in Christ they will gain no hold on you.

Galatians 5:1 "It is for freedom that Christ has set us free. Stand firm, then, and do not let yourselves be burdened again by a yoke of slavery."

Being a slave to Christ actually means being free, so do not go back to being a slave to anything else. That is when you will get entangled by addiction.

Your freedom has already been paid for in full on Calvary. Everything that once bound you is under subjection to the Lord. You made bail when you accepted Jesus as your Lord and Savior. The gavel of God has dropped, and He says you are free!

Learn about freedom from:

Mary Magdalene

Her Testimony...

People would gossip about me and my struggle with demons. I had a darkness surrounding my heart, and I did not think I would ever be free. But one day I ran into a man named Jesus and He cured me of the evil spirits that I had dealt with for so long. He made me free. From that point forward I followed Him. Where He went, I went. I sat under His teaching and began to learn all about my worth and my value. I learned about God the Father and listened to the parables that Jesus spoke. I was a new person.

I could feel in my spirit it was time to anoint Jesus with the precious perfume that was in my alabaster box. I heard He was in town eating at Simon the leper's house, so I made my way to Him. I could feel the people casting judgment. I could see their hateful glances toward me. I could hear them whispering about my past. I pressed on. I fought the thoughts of unworthiness and doubt. I refused to focus on my past and focused in on all that mattered. I focused on making my way to Jesus. And with every step I could feel redemption, I could feel the pain of my past being healed, I could feel forgiveness; my soul finally felt its true worth.

I poured out the alabaster box and anointed Him, my precious Savior. I washed His feet with my tears of gratitude and dried them with my hair. They did not understand, but that did not matter. All that mattered at that moment was Jesus and me.

At that moment, I poured out my past to God and let Him redeem me. I poured out my present so He could use me. I poured out my future to show I trusted Him always and forever in everything. And because I poured myself out to Him I got to be there for the two most important times in His life. I was there for His crucifixion and His resurrection. I saw what my redemption cost Him. I saw the price He paid for humanity. I heard Him say that it was finished.

I thought I would never see Him again. My precious Savior had died. I went to the tomb to be near my Lord and noticed His body was gone. I wept, not knowing where they took my Lord. I just wanted to be near Him. Then the gardener asked why I was crying, and I told him. But then He said my name and I recognized His voice! It was no gardener at all it was Jesus, my

Teacher, my Lord!

I got to be the first to see that my Redeemer lives! Death could not hold Him down!

When I gave it all to the Lord, I was free.

Her breaking point: Freedom through Christ

Give all of yourself to God and all of you will be free! Just like we see in this testimony, we have to let go of everything that hinders and tries to bind us to be free. She had to let go of past mistakes to be free. She had to refuse to listen to other people's opinions to be free. She had to get to Jesus to be free. She found out the truth about Jesus and never went back to chains. She let the truth of who Jesus is break every chain.

The lack of knowledge causes fear; the knowledge of truth causes freedom. How much truth do you know?

Do you know what the word says about your life? Do you know what it says about your purpose? Do you know what it says about your future? Do you know what it says about love? Do you know what it says about your healing? Do you know what it says about your goals? Do you know what it says about your deliverance? Do you know what it says about your circumstance?

How much you know AND believe determines how free you can be.

God can free you from anything and everything at any time.

John 8:26 "So if the Son sets you free, you will be free indeed."

If He has freed you from it, then you are indeed free. Trust in that! Trust in Him for your freedom!

To be beautifully broken is to let God make you free.

You are beautifully free! When anything tries to bind you, tell yourself:

I AM BEAUTIFULLY FREE!

Chapter Six

Beautifully Healed

At one point or another in your life, you have probably been in need of healing. Maybe you have needed healing in your body or healing in your mind. Maybe you have needed God to heal you not only physically and mentally, but spiritually as well. The great thing about God's healing is that it covers it all. Everything that needs healing can be healed by Him.

Broken hearts to broken bodies, He heals them. If you have been hurt, He can heal you. If you have been offended, He can heal you. If you are sick, He can heal you. No matter where you need healing in your life, He is able to heal you.

Isaiah 53:5 "But he was wounded for our transgressions, he was bruised for our iniquities: the chastisement of our peace was upon him, and with his stripes we are healed."

By His stripes, you ARE healed. His stripes are to make you healthy and whole. His stripes are to bring an end to your pain and your sickness. His stripes are to make things right in our bodies and in our lives. His stripes repair. His stripes restore.

1 Peter 2:24 "Who his own self bare our sins in his own body on the tree, that we, being dead to sins, should live unto righteousness: by whose stripes ye were healed."

By whose stripes you WERE healed. His stripes have already taken care of your healing. Your condition does not have to be chronic. Your condition has a cure! Jesus is your hope. Jesus is your cure! By His stripes, you are healed.

If there is a physical sickness in your body where the healing has not manifested, keep the faith. Keep fighting for your faith. Every pain you feel, confess His stripes. Every doctor's report, confess His stripes. If there is depression that tries to take hold of your life, confess His stripes. If you are wounded in your spirit, confess His stripes. If your mind is raging, confess His stripes. Never stop confessing His stripes.

God does not wish evil against you. That sickness, pain, and hurt is not from Him.

God is good and does only good.

3 John 1:2 "Beloved, I wish above all things that thou mayest prosper and be in health, even as thy soul prospereth."

You are God's beloved; He wants you to prosper and be in health. There is not one place in your life that the Lord can't heal. If there is any place broken He wants to make it whole.

Isaiah 54:17 "No weapon that is formed against thee shall prosper."

There will be cancers formed against you. There will be pain and hurt formed against you. There will be offense thrown your way. But they SHALL NOT PROSPER in Jesus name. What shall prosper in you is the Word of God and it says you are healed. It says you can be made whole. Trust Him, no matter how you are feeling. He will not leave you. He will see you through every step of the way. Your healing is right around the corner; do not give up now.

Matthew 9:22 "Jesus turned and saw her. "Take heart, daughter," he said, "your faith has healed you." And the woman was healed at that moment."

Take heart! Your faith can make all of the difference. Do you believe He can heal you? Do you believe He is willing to heal you? Will you let Him make you whole? Let your faith answer, "YES!"

There are numerous stories in the Bible where Jesus healed the sick, and He is still healing the sick today. Healing requires faith. Put your faith in Him and do not lean on your own understanding. Do not lean on the doctor's report or the pain. Trust in the Lord with all your heart and remember His ways are higher than ours. Do not lose hope! Jesus is still the miracle worker you need Him to be.

Learn about the miracle of being healed from:

The Woman with the Issue of Blood

Her Testimony...

People have always identified me with my weakness. They never call me by my name, but they love to refer to my "issue." What they so casually called my issue was my life, it was something with which I struggled with every day for 12 long years. To them, it was so little but it was on my mind constantly, and the pain was unbearable at times. I couldn't eat, I couldn't sleep, it was horrible! My sickness caused me to go from doctor to doctor. I spent my entire life savings and nothing helped. I actually was worse than when I started.

The worst part of my disease was that it made me barren; I couldn't have children. Oh, how I wanted kids so badly, but my issue affected my production. I would see my friends get married and have children, and I would smile on the outside, but on the inside I was jealous, I was mad, I was frustrated! When would it be my turn? When would my miracle happen? When would my breakthrough show up?

Then out of nowhere, I started hearing the whispers about a miracle man named Jesus. They said He was coming to my city. I knew this might be my last chance. I knew I just couldn't lie in my bed and wait anymore; I had to get up and make something happen.

I mustered all my strength and made it to the door. As I walked out of my house, the crowds pushed passed me. By the time I made it to see Him, hundreds, maybe thousands, of people had already gathered. My energy gone, the pain excruciating, I dropped to my knees. All I could do now...was crawl. As I crawled and fought my way to Jesus, people stepped and spit on me. They kicked and cussed me, but I would not stop, I could not be stopped!

I finally made it to Jesus. I couldn't speak; I couldn't stand...all I could do was reach up and touch His robe, oh but when I did!!!! Something amazing happened! This issue that I had carried for 12 years was gone, completely gone! I was healed. Jesus made me whole!

Her Breaking Point: Receiving healing only Christ could give

Jesus is no respecter of persons, and He is willing and able to do the same for you. It is God's will for you to be healed. He is still the Healer. He is still the Way Maker. Make your way to Jesus, touch the hem of His garment through your praise, worship, prayer, thanksgiving, and receive your healing.

To be beautifully broken is to be healed by faith.

You are beautifully healed! When pain attacks your mind and your body, tell your flesh:

I AM BEAUTIFULLY HEALED!

Chapter Seven

Beautifully Happy

It seems that happiness is a rare trait these days. Everyone is looking for happiness, but they are looking in all the wrong places. Where do you look to find your happiness? Do you look to the things of this world to make you happy or do you find your joy in the Lord? If you find your happiness in the Lord, then your happiness can't be taken away, not by people or circumstances because the joy of the Lord is your strength.

1 John 2:17 "The world and its desires pass away, but whoever does the will of God lives forever."

1 Samuel 2:1 (God's Word Translation) "My heart finds joy in the LORD. My head is lifted to the LORD. My mouth mocks my enemies. I rejoice because you saved [me]."

If your happiness is found in the world then it can be taken away, but find a happy heart in the Lord and no one can touch it. This does not mean you won't have hard times; it just means you can make it through intact. A life of joy will prevent depression and anger. A life of joy brings joy to others. Happiness can come in many ways, but one of the truest forms it comes is through a thankful heart. A thankful person is a happy person. Be thankful for everything even the little things, and you will find joy.

Proverbs 15:15 "All the days of the oppressed are wretched, but the cheerful heart has a continual feast."

You do not have to live oppressed, choose to be happy and you will have a continual harvest. You will have a continual harvest because you will see more things as a harvest. Look at the bright side of life, and you will have a continual feast in your life. Have the courage to be an optimist.

Proverbs 17:22 "A cheerful heart is good medicine, but a crushed spirit dries up the bones."

James 1:2 "Consider it pure joy, my brothers and sisters, whenever you face trials of many kinds."

You will still have rough days, you will still face trials, and you will still have obstacles to overcome, but with joy, you will see the purpose of what you go through with spiritual eyes. There is a reason for everything you go through; let joy be your guide through it all. It's hard to break someone when they are full of the joy of the Lord. You can't keep a joyful person down. They just get back up, dust themselves off, and they learn from their trials.

Learn about finding happiness from:

Leah

Her Testimony…

I have always been compared to my beautiful sister, Rachel, but I am the one known for weak eyes. I am the eldest daughter of Laban. I am Leah.

I was never going to be as beautiful as Rachel and have the prospects that she had. She had always been favored and I had always been unfortunate. Then one day along came Jacob. Of course, he saw my sister first and fell in love with her.

Jacob worked seven long years for my father and in return asked for Rachel's hand in marriage. My father agreed to this, and soon there was a wedding. But not Rachel's, it was to be mine. My father began to prepare me for the wedding to be Jacob's bride. Of course, I wanted to be married to Jacob but not like this. I wanted him to love me. But I went along with my father's plan anyway. I was to trick Jacob and wear a veil so that he would think he was marrying Rachel. How embarrassing it was to know that the only way I could get Jacob to marry me was to pretend to be Rachel. My father must have thought this was the only way he could marry me off. I felt like such a disappointment.

When Jacob realized he had married me, he was very upset, to say the least and again I was a disappointment. He went to my father and worked another seven years for Rachel. So now I felt like I was in competition again with my sister and she would always win.

I saw that Jacob loved my sister more than he would ever love me. Did he even love me at all? My heart ached for my husband's love. The Lord saw this, and He opened up my womb. I gave birth to a healthy baby boy and named him Reuben - the Lord has seen my misery; surely my husband will love me now. Then I conceived again, and again, and again. My fourth son I named Judah because this time I will praise the Lord. Then my handmaiden bore another son to my husband and me. I called him Asher, because now I am happy, and the other women shall call me happy.

It was when I praised the Lord that I found peace in my marriage. It was when I found joy in the Lord that made my life happy.

I continued in my praise, and the Lord gave me two more children.

My last son I named Zebulun because God had given me a precious gift and my husband will treat me with honor. My last child was a girl, and I named her Dinah because the Lord had vindicated me. It wasn't until I praised God that I felt uplifted and justified in my marriage.

My joy and my praise made a difference!

Her Breaking Point: Choosing Joy

Your joy and your praise will make a difference in your life. Leah had every reason to be unhappy, but God kept showing her mercy and grace and kept blessing her with children to show her that she could be happy. Happiness is a choice. Make up in your mind that you will be happy. Be happy that God has breathed life into you. That very breath you breathe is a beautiful gift that can bring joy.

Abraham Lincoln once said, "We can complain because the rose bushes have thorns or rejoice because thorn bushes have roses." You can complain because your life has been hard or you can rejoice because you have a life. All of those things that happened to you can make you stronger.

Philippians 4:11-13 "I have learned to be content whatever the circumstances. I know what it is to be in need, and I know what it is to have plenty. I have learned the secret of being content in any and every situation, whether well fed or hungry, whether living in plenty or in want. I can do all this through him who gives me strength."

Be content with where you are, knowing that the Lord is in control. You can be content without settling. He will give you the strength to be happy. The pursuit of happiness is in God's Word. Find your joy in Him!

Ecclesiastes 3:12 "I know that there is nothing better for people than to be happy and to do good while they live."

Psalm 100:2 "Serve the LORD with gladness: come before his presence with singing."

To be beautifully broken is to find joy in the Lord.

You are beautifully happy in Christ!

When sadness tries to overtake you and the weight of this world tries to weigh you down, tell yourself:

I AM BEAUTIFULLY HAPPY!

Chapter Eight

Beautifully Different

When you get saved, a transformation of the heart takes place. This transformation of the heart is meant to roll over into every aspect of your life. You are not meant to be the same person after you have received Christ. God will teach you a new and living way. You were never meant to fit in. You were always meant to be different. Let God transform the way you think, talk, and act. There is a better way to live. There is a different way to live.

Ezekiel 36:26 "I will give you a new heart and put a new spirit in you; I will remove from you your heart of stone and give you a heart of flesh."

People around you will notice a difference in you, and that is a good thing because you should be different. When you allow the transformation to take over your life, you will have "haters" so be prepared to push past all of the negative people. You might have to leave behind some old relationships because they are unhealthy for you. Some of your friends might not understand the new you. Get involved with people who are trying to live a transformed life just like you are. As iron sharpens iron so, a friend will sharpen a friend.

Same is true for bad company. If you keep bad company around you, they will corrupt you. It is very hard to pull someone up and far too easy to pull someone down. Allow God to make you strong. That way you can keep yourself up and help others.

John 15:19 "If you belonged to the world, it would love you as its own. As it is, you do not belong to the world, but I have chosen you out of the world. That is why the world hates you."

You do not belong to this world; you belong to God. Let Him fight your battles while you fight for your faith. It will take great faith to stay different. You will have to let God transform the way you think and the way you respond to things. To stay on the straight and narrow path, to endure this race, you are going to have to accept that you are different, and you have to do things differently. You can't act like the world acts and do what the world does.

Matthew 7: 13-14 "Enter through the narrow gate. For wide is the gate and broad is the road that leads to destruction, and many enter through it. But small is the gate and narrow the road that leads to life, and only a few find it."

Being different is a good thing. Following the Word of God will make you different from your peers. God has separated you from the crowd and called you His own.

2 Corinthians 6:17 "Come out from them and be separate, says the Lord. Touch no unclean thing, and

I will receive you."

This is how you can be separate:

1 Thessalonians 4:3-7 "It is God's will that you should be sanctified: that you should avoid sexual immorality; that each of you should learn to control your own body in a way that is holy and honorable, not in passionate lust like the pagans, who do not know God; and that in this matter no one should wrong or take advantage of a brother or sister. The Lord will punish all those who commit such sins, as we told you and warned you before. For God did not call us to be impure, but to live a holy life."

God is calling you to be different; He is calling you to be pure and live a holy life. This will be a challenge but will be worth every effort you put in. In this life, you will get what you put into it.

Learn about being different from:

Esther

Her Testimony...

My story began when my cousin and I heard the news that Queen Vashti had been relinquished of her duties as queen. Now there was a search in all the land for someone to take her place to be the new queen.

Mordecai thought it would be a good idea if I were the new queen. But that would be impossible, right? There were thousands of young women who wanted to be queen. How could a Jewish orphan ever be queen? I was different than all of them. King Xerxes saw that I was different, and he saw that I cared about different things than the other women.

I found favor with King Xerxes, and I became his bride. A great banquet took place where everyone celebrated our new marriage. This palace was now my home. The King was now my husband. Mordecai soon came to me with news that he had overheard two officers plotting to kill the king, my husband. I quickly reported this to the king and his life was saved.

During this time a man named Haman was honored by my husband and declared higher than the other officials. People were to bow to him on the streets, but there was one man who refused, Mordecai. This ate Haman up inside and had him detesting all Jews. Haman went to the King and requested that these disobedient Jews be slaughtered. And it was decreed that all Jews be put to death. Mordecai sent word to me about the decree. I could not believe it. God's people, my people, my family were to be destroyed.

My king did not know that I was a Jew. I hid this from him because Mordecai told me to, but now we are all to be put to death. I could hide the fact that I was different and maybe be saved, but my people would still be slaughtered.

I had to speak up for my family and for God's people. The only way to do this was to approach the king. But the king had not asked to see me in thirty days. I remembered what he did to Vashti when she displeased him. If I approached him and he did not extend the golden scepter toward me, I would be put to death!

Mordecai reminded me that perhaps I was chosen for such a time as this, so I made a choice. I would fight. I would stand up for my family, and if I were to die, I would willingly die.

When I approached the king, I could feel my heart jumping inside my chest. This was it; this was my chance. He extended the scepter toward me, and I could finally breathe. I walked toward him and asked for his presence at a dinner I would prepare for him and Haman. He was quite confused at my request for Haman to join us. But I had a plan.

We had one dinner then I requested another. This time, I would make known that I am a Jew, and I would petition for my people and my family.

As we sat at dinner, the king asked me what my request was. I mustered all of my courage, strength, and faith in the Lord and answered, "Oh king, if I have found favor with you, and it pleases you, grant me my life and spare my people." I revealed I was a Jew and the very decree he ordered was against my people.

This angered the King and he asked who would do such a thing, and I answered, "Haman." So the king sent Haman to his death. But that was not the end of my fight. What about my people?

I petitioned once again to the king to reverse the order set against the Jews, and it was done. Not only was I saved but my household was saved, my friends were saved, my people were saved! I lived a pure life; I embraced the fact that I was different in the Lord, and it made a difference in the people around me.

Her Breaking Point: Being different than everyone else and receiving favor from the Lord

Step into the will of God by being different. Be holy in an unholy generation; be pure when everyone else is impure. Be righteous among the unrighteous. Be beautifully broken among the broken beautiful. Your life will impact others when you are different. When you live differently than the world, you can change the world.

To be beautifully broken is to let the Lord make you different than the world.

You are beautifully different!

When the world does not "get" you, remind your flesh and tell yourself:

I AM BEAUTIFULLY DIFFERENT.

Chapter Nine

Beautifully Approved

Have you ever sought after someone's approval? There might have been times in your life where you have wished for approval from a mother and father, a teacher, a coach, a boss, or a friend. Seeking after approval is common to all man. It is normal to want everyone to approve of you. But the truth is, not everyone will approve of you, no matter how hard you try. Do not please man at the expense of displeasing God. Your first priority in everything is to seek God's approval. Let the Lord validate you and what you do.

2 Corinthians 10:18 "For it is not one who commends himself who is approved, but the one who the Lord commends."

Too many times we choose to hear the voice of our critics over the voice of the Lord. There could be hundreds of people that encourage you and one negative critic. Chances are, you often choose to hear only the critic. The approval that man gives is very limited and temporary, but the approval of the Lord can last all eternity. There are hundreds of choices that you will have to make every day. What is the deciding factor in your life, God or man? Your first action before every choice you make should be to ask the Lord if He approves. If God gives you the go ahead, then you know you are good to go.

2 Timothy 2:15 "Do your best to present yourself to God as one approved, a worker who does not need to be ashamed and who correctly handles the Word of truth."

God has officially approved you to be blessed when you seek His approval. Learn to please the Lord in everything you do. Pleasing the Lord will always be better for you than pleasing people. The benefits to pleasing the Lord are endless and are forever.

Hebrews 11:4 "By faith he was approved as a righteous man, because God approves his gifts…"

By faith, you are approved. Faith will make you want to live a righteous life before God. Let God approve of your gifts. Understand that God's approval is based upon the heart and not upon ability. Give God your heart to search. Let Him approve of what you say and what you do and even what you wear. Let Him show you what He approves of and then follow the guidelines He gives.

The world checks your credit for approval. To get approved for things in the world like a car, a house, or a loan of any kind, they will have to check your credit. To get approved in the Kingdom of God, they check Jesus' credit. His credit says you have been preapproved to be the head and not the tail. His credit says you have been preapproved by His blood to have every need met. His

Col 3:23
Whatever you do

82

credit says you have been preapproved to be blessed.

Questions that should always be at the forefront of your heart:

Does this please the Lord?

Will God approve?

Hosea 4:8 "They set up kings without my consent; they choose princes without my approval. With their silver and gold, they make idols for themselves to their own destruction."

When people do things without God and without His approval, it causes destruction. Have you ever placed anything in your life as a "king" without God's consent? Have you allowed anything or anyone into your life without God's approval? God is not trying to steal the things that you enjoy; He is trying to save you from destruction.

Learn about being beautifully approved from:

Deborah

Her Testimony...

I was called to do many things that, at the time, only men were approved to do. I did not have to be approved by man; I was approved by God to do what I did. I lived an upright life before God, and He allowed me to be a judge for the people. I had proved myself to God that I would be His vessel, and He used me to lead an army to war. A woman leading an army was not very common, and I am sure there were naysayers about my ability in the crowd. I did not care though because I knew I was approved with the approval that mattered.

God showed me what had to be done. He showed me what He approved of during the time of war. I spoke to Barak, who was the General of the Army. I told him what the Lord had said. He would agree to do as the Lord had said only if I would come with him into battle. I could have been afraid to go into a man's war, but I knew whose consent I had, so I went with him into this battle that looked impossible to win and won. I sought the Lord's approval over man's opinion, and God gave the victory. I gave God my ear, and He gave me instruction. I was approved because I chose to listen to God. I let the things that pleased God please my soul.

Her Breaking Point: Knowing God's approval is what gains the victory

Get God's approval on your relationships, career choices, and everything else you do and it will save you from a lot of trouble. Please God first and He will give you the victory. When you seek God's approval first, He will give you the approval from men that you need to be successful in this world. God can change the hearts of men for your favor.

1 Thessalonians 2:4 "On the contrary, we speak as those approved by God to be entrusted with the

gospel. We are not trying to please people but God, who tests our hearts."

To be beautifully broken is to seek God's approval first.

When man does not approve, tell yourself whose approval really matters and declare:

I AM BEAUTIFULLY APPROVED!

Chapter Ten

Beautifully Wise

Wisdom is one of the most important things that you can receive as a believer. To be wise is a beautiful thing and receiving wisdom is entirely up to you. To gain wisdom, you must first receive knowledge of the Word of God. It's important that you understand that it is not just about how much you know, it's about how much you believe of what you know. You not only have to know and believe the Word of God, but you also have to apply it. It is in the application of your knowledge that you become wise.

The world can give you book smarts, but only God and His Word can give you supernatural wisdom. Gaining wisdom is crucial to your faith. If you weave the Word into every part of your life, you will have wisdom in every part of your life. To be wise, you must first understand that everything in your life must be checked by God and His Word. When you do not know, when you are unsure, and when you do not understand, always go to His Word. Sometimes you may not get the answer you want, or it may seem you get no answer at all. That is when your faith has to kick in and trust God because He knows the beginning from the end. His wisdom is greater than our understanding, so it is wise to let your faith help you make it through when you do not understand.

You do not have to understand everything to be wise. You just have to trust in God's Word. God wants you to hide His Word in your heart so He can guide you, if you know His Word then you know His heart. Seeking His heart will give you knowledge and wisdom. Knowledge earned and applied is wisdom gained and wisdom gained is rewarded.

Proverbs 9:12 "If you are wise, your wisdom will reward you; if you are a mocker, you alone will suffer."

Godly wisdom is irreplaceable and invaluable to every believer. Not only are you rewarded for your efforts in wisdom but you are also saved from terrible amounts of trouble when you apply wisdom in every circumstance. Wisdom will keep you out of sticky situations. Continually follow the Word and obey what it says; that is wisdom. The Word has all the information you require to gain the wisdom that you desperately need to thrive. God has given us instructions on how to become wise in His Word. You just have to read His Word and value what you are reading.

Psalm 119:105 "Your word is a lamp to my feet and a light to my path."

Will you let His Word be your answer?

Will you let His Word guide you?

Will you keep and obey His Word?

Will you let His Word be the final say?

The only one who can decide the answers to those questions is you. When you receive a Word from the Lord, guard it in your heart because there will always be an attack on the Word that you receive. The devil will try to steal the Word of God from your heart by tempting you and giving you trials and tribulations. Never give in to the doubt, and never give into the confusion the devil tries to stir up. God is a God of clarity and not confusion. The devil is the author of confusion. Whenever you are confused, seek God's counsel because He can clarify things for you. Things become clear when you see through God's eyes.

Psalm 119:11 "I have hidden your word in my heart that I might not sin against you."

Proverbs 4:23 "Above all else, guard your heart, for everything you do flows from it."

Hide the Word in your heart and then guard it with all your might. Guard the promises God has spoken to you. Remind yourself daily of His Word. Find the verses that apply to your everyday situations and use them. Live, move, and have your being in Him and His Word.

Ecclesiastes 7:12 "Wisdom is a shelter as money is a shelter, but the advantage of knowledge is this: Wisdom preserves those who have it."

Wisdom will preserve your very life when you use it. Wisdom has the ability to preserve your marriage, finances, and family. Do everything in your power to gain as much wisdom as you can. Be careful with whom you surround yourself because the Word tells us that if we walk with the wise, we will become wise. However, if we surround ourselves with the unwise, we will have trouble.

Proverbs 13:20 "Walk with the wise and become wise; associate with fools and get in trouble."

The world has plenty of trouble to offer. You do not need anyone else's trouble creeping into your life. Be very careful of the relationships you allow. Wisdom will teach you who is in and who should be out of your life. It will show you who is good for you and who is not. It will teach you what relationships are beneficial and what relationships are hindrances. Let wisdom be your instructor and God the orchestrator. When you do, God will give you the wisdom to speak.

Proverbs 16:23 "The heart of the wise teacheth his mouth, and addeth learning to his lips."

It matters what you say. Speak with wisdom and not emotion. Allow wisdom to have its perfect work in you by giving God control. Give God control of what you speak. Do not speak out of anger and hurt. Speak the truth in love and that is wisdom. Stay silent when directed by the Lord and that is wisdom. Be wise in everything, including your speech. Your tongue will be unruly only if you let it. You have control over what you say and what you do not say.

What are you speaking?

Is it wisdom or is it opinion?

Is it wisdom or is it emotion?

Is it wisdom or is it anger?

Give God your words so He can make them wise.

Learn about being beautifully wise from:

The Prophet Anna

Her Testimony…

I was married a short seven years before I became a widow; my heart was broken. I felt the pain that loss causes. I took those seven years and learned from them. Instead of allowing my loss to push me away from God, I allowed it to draw me closer. I stayed a widow the rest of my days and decided to devote my time to the Lord. I was now very old, but the Lord increased my knowledge of Him and gave me wisdom to become a prophet. Day in and day out I would seek His face. I would worship, fast, and pray day and night. I sought the Lord and His righteousness. I concerned myself with His Word and His will.

I grew close to the Lord, and He gave me supernatural wisdom. I let wisdom instruct me and direct my path and that wisdom positioned me to meet the baby named

Jesus, who would grow to be the Redeemer of us all. He would redeem the lost and bring salvation to all who believed in all generations. I thanked God for Jesus and knew in my heart that redemption had come for Jerusalem. Wisdom kept me and wisdom taught me, and most importantly introduced me to my precious Savior.

Her Breaking Point: Growing in wisdom and being directed by wisdom

Wisdom will place you where you need to be in the right place at the right time. Just like Anna, you will have to seek the Lord for your wisdom. To achieve wisdom, you must be willing to be taught by the Lord. Anna placed herself to receive wisdom from the Lord by her worship, prayer, and fasting. She listened to instruction and let the Lord give her the Words to speak. She prepared herself to meet Jesus by seeking the wisdom of the Lord.

When you are wise, you will prepare your heart for the days to come. Wisdom will make you want to prepare properly. Wisdom will prepare your heart to receive, your eyes to see, and your ears to hear what the Spirit is saying. Wisdom gives no place to distractions and the weights of this world. It places itself in the presence of the Lord and focuses on what really matters. Wisdom will make you powerful in the Kingdom of God.

Ecclesiastes 7:19 "Wisdom makes one wise person more powerful than ten rulers in a city."

Ecclesiastes 9:18 "Wisdom is better than weapons of war, but one sinner destroys much good."

Wisdom is what you should hope to attain every day of your life no matter what your age. Wisdom can be ever increasing and is a spiritual weapon against the enemy.

You do not have to run this race without wisdom. Wisdom can be found at every turn in the pages of His Word. This life is not pointless, and you do not have to be aimless. You must learn what you are fighting for, and wisdom will teach you just that. It will teach you why you fight and why your life is worth fighting for. Follow His commands that are found in His Word and you will be wiser than your adversary. Rightly divide the Word and you will be able to rightly divide life.

1 Corinthians 9:26 "Therefore I do not run like someone running aimlessly; I do not fight like a boxer beating the air."

Psalm 119:98 "Your commands are always with me and make me wiser than my enemies."

It is time to stop beating the air and time to start hitting the mark through wisdom.

To be beautifully broken is to fight for wisdom.

You are beautifully wise!

When this life tries to confuse you, go to God's Word,
get wisdom and declare:

I AM BEAUTIFULLY WISE!

Chapter Eleven

Beautifully Filled

You do not have to live an empty life. God wants your life to be full. You have to empty yourself of everything you have so God can fill you with all that He has. What God wants to fill you with is greater than an adrenaline rush, greater than a high from a drug, and greater than intoxication from alcohol. He wants to fill you with a blessed assurance. He can fill you with the peace you need to make it through the day and fill you with hope for every tomorrow.

If you have had a loss in your life and feel that deep emptiness that loss can leave behind, God wants to fill you with the peace that passes all understanding. Or if you have experienced any lack of peace in any area of your life for any reason, God wants to be your peace at all times.

Philippians 4:7 "And the peace of God, which transcends all understanding, will guard your hearts and your minds in Christ Jesus."

2 Thessalonians 3:17 "Now may the Lord of peace himself give you peace at all times and in every way. The Lord be with all of you."

When you find peace, you will find rest. If you trust the Lord with all your heart in everything, God will fill you with peace. He has given us His Word so that we may find peace for whatever we face.

Not only does He want to fill you with peace. He wants to fill you with hope; a hope that is an anchor to your soul, a hope that is forever. Your hope is always in Jesus. When your hope is in Jesus, you can push through even the most difficult of circumstances.

Lamentations 3:20-22 "I will never forget this awful time, as I grieve over my loss. Yet I still dare to hope when I remember this: The faithful love of the Lord never ends! His mercies never cease."

You may have had some awful times in your life, but your life is not over. Dare to hope. Dare to expect great things from God. Do bad things happen? Yes, but God can fill you with hope for a better day. With that hope, He wants to give you power.

Romans 15:13 "May the God of hope fill you with all joy and peace as you trust in him, so that you may overflow with hope by the power of the Holy Spirit."

For every loss, every heartache, and every pain there is a comforter. God has given His Spirit to comfort you, help you, and teach you. God wants to fill you with the same power that raised Christ from the dead. God wants us to be filled with the Holy Spirit so that we can discern what to do in every situation. The Holy Spirit has been given to us as a gift to be our Comforter, our Helper, our

Teacher, our Guide, our Intercessor, our Counselor, our Advocate, our Wisdom, our Covering and our Power. Find all the answers to the questions you may have about the Holy Spirit in the Word. You can't go wrong when you stick with the Word. His Word is alive and true, and I pray He reveals the gift of the Holy Spirit to you.

The Holy Spirit is the Spirit of God that dwells in you, which is given as a gift. The Spirit of God has always been, even before the world.

Genesis 1:2 "And the earth was without form, and void; and darkness was upon the face of the deep. And the Spirit of God moved upon the face of the waters."

Who is the Holy Spirit to you? The Spirit is...

- Your Wisdom

- Your Understanding

- Your Counselor

- Your Might

- Your Knowledge

- Your Covering

- Your Protection

- Your Advocate

- Your Teacher

- Your Power

As you can see, the Spirit does so much for you and has the potential to help you beyond belief.

Is the Holy Spirit for you today? YES!

The Holy Spirit counsels us and, now that Christ has been glorified, the Spirit is for all who want it. Whatever good God has, He wants for all His people, to all generations, which includes you!

The Holy Spirit no longer has to depart from you when you stumble, but now because of the redemptive power of the blood of Jesus Christ, the Holy Spirit can help pick you back up. The Holy Spirit can correct you and instruct you. You just have to be willing to listen. Do not quench the Spirit by refusing to listen.

What is the difference between 'sealed' and 'filled' with the Holy Spirit?

'Seal' means 'perfect closure.' When we are saved, we have perfect closure on our sin and entrance into Heaven through Jesus.

'Filled' means to 'take up all the space and make full.' That's what happens when you are filled with the power of the Spirit. You are made full.

Ephesians 4:30 "And grieve not the Holy Spirit of God, whereby ye are sealed unto the day of redemption."

Ephesians speaks of the transformation that is made when we accept salvation through Jesus Christ. We are sealed with the Spirit, allowing us entrance into Heaven.

Acts 19:2-6 "He said unto them, Have ye received the Holy Ghost since ye believed? And they said unto him, we have not so much as heard whether there be any Holy Ghost. And he said unto them, unto what then were ye baptized? And they said, Unto John's baptism. Then said Paul, John verily baptized with the baptism of repentance, saying unto the people, that they should believe on him which should come after him, that is, on Christ Jesus. When they heard this, they were baptized in the name of the Lord Jesus. And when Paul had laid his hands upon them, the Holy Ghost came on them; and they spake with tongues, and prophesied."

Paul speaks of the indwelling of the Holy Spirit after salvation and the sealing of the Spirit in our lives.

The filling of the Holy Spirit is for us after salvation to give us power and victory while we are on earth. The sealing of the Spirit in our lives is only the beginning. Being filled with the Holy Spirit is to help us endure this race with victories all along the way, not just at the end.

How can I receive the Holy Spirit?

Ask for it!

Who can receive the Holy Spirit?

Anyone who believes! The only prerequisite is salvation through Jesus Christ.

The Holy Spirit is a gift; it cannot be bought. The Spirit is not something you pay for because Christ has already paid for it.

Acts 8:18 & 20 "And when Simon saw that through laying on of the apostles' hands the Holy Ghost was given, he offered them money, But Peter said unto him, Thy money perish with thee, because thou hast thought that the gift of God may be purchased with money."

Acts 2:38 "Then Peter said unto them, Repent, and be baptized every one of you in the name of Jesus Christ for the remission of sins, and ye shall receive the gift of the Holy Ghost."

Acts 10:45 "And they of the circumcision which believed were astonished, as many as came with Peter, because that on the Gentiles also was poured out the gift of the Holy Ghost."

Even Gentiles are able to receive the gift of the Holy Spirit.

Luke 11:13 "If ye then, being evil, know how to give good gifts unto your children: how much more shall [your] heavenly Father give the Holy Spirit to them that ask him?"

God is willing and able to fill you with the gift of the Holy Spirit! God is eager to bless you with this gift. Are you just as eager to receive it? You may ask what all is involved in receiving the Holy Spirit and what should you expect after receiving the gift.

These are the things you can expect from the Holy Spirit:

- Comfort

- Hope

- Peace

- Power

- To be led

- Circumcision of the heart

- To be taught

- Joy

- Boldness

- Your very own prayer language

The Holy Spirit can give you the words to speak when you pray. When you do not know what to say, the Spirit can give you the utterance.

Jude 1:20 "But ye, beloved, building up yourselves on your most holy faith, praying in the Holy Ghost."

1 Corinthians 14: 15 "What is it then? I will pray with the spirit, and I will pray with the understanding also: I will sing with the spirit, and I will sing with the understanding also."

Why is praying in the Holy Spirit so important?

Praying in the Holy Spirit is praying for God's perfect will to be done. It prevents our flesh from getting in the way.

Praying in the Holy Spirit allows us to pray for things we do not even know about yet.

Praying in the Holy Spirit is powerful.

The Holy Spirit is supernatural.

How do I begin to pray in the Holy Spirit?

Your prayer language is part of the gift of the Holy Spirit. Use your voice but give God control. Praying in the Spirit moves the flesh out the way so the Spirit can do the talking.

God wants to not only give you your very own prayer language, but also fill you with the fruits and gifts of the Spirit. Within the Spirit, there are so many blessings attached that will not only fill you but will overflow you.

Galatians 5:22-23 "But the fruit of the Spirit is love, joy, peace, longsuffering, gentleness, goodness, faith, Meekness, temperance: against such there is no law."

FRUITS OF THE SPIRIT

- Love

- Joy

- Peace

- Longsuffering

- Gentleness

- Goodness

- Faith

- Meekness

- Temperance

The fruits of the Spirit equip you and help you better operate in the gifts of the Spirit.

GIFTS OF THE SPIRIT

- Wisdom

- Word of Knowledge

- Faith

- Healing

- Working of Miracles

- Prophecy

- Discerning Spirits

- Diverse Tongues

- Interpretation of Tongues

1 Corinthians 14:1 "Follow the way of love and eagerly desire gifts of the Spirit..."

The gifts of God enable you to do the work of God and edify His people. All the gifts are important and given by God to each individual how He sees fit. Not everyone will have the same gift, but everyone does have a gift when filled with the Spirit. He will give you what you need, and He will sustain you by His Spirit.

The Holy Spirit is part of making sure you are adding to your faith and making every effort to draw closer to God.

The Holy Spirit will help you add to your faith and gives you gifts that the scripture says help to sustain you. The Holy Spirit helps you to see and not be blind to the things of God. In order to fully understand like God, you will need the Spirit of God. The Spirit helps you to better understand His Word and His will. The Spirit will teach you what man cannot.

The Holy Spirit is bearing record for you and accounts for you. Even when the devil accuses you, he cannot put you to death because God is on your side! He has given you the Holy Spirit to keep you.

Learn about being filled from:

Elizabeth

Her Testimony…

My heart ached for a child of my own. My husband, Zechariah, and I longed for the day of conceiving. We thought that day had passed. We grew old and the season for having children was over for me. Or so I thought. God had other plans. The Lord sent an angel to tell my husband that we would have a child, and so it was. Soon I was pregnant and full of joy because God opened my womb and took the brokenness away. I was in a wonderful season in my life.

Things could not have gotten better. Everything was lining up so beautifully, and my life was truly blessed. I was sitting outside one day when I heard Mary call out and approach me. I loved seeing Mary but this time, something was different. I saw there was a glow not only on her face but upon her spirit as well. The child that was growing within my womb leaped for joy, I felt this joy radiate through my soul and was gloriously filled with the Holy Spirit. I saw that the baby Mary was carrying was the blessed of the Lord. I was blessed that such a favored woman of the Lord would come and visit me. I rejoiced with her, and she rejoiced with me. My spirit was full within me. The Lord was doing a mighty work, and I was blessed to be filled with such a wonderful gift to be a part of it! My life was good and got even better with the Spirit!

Her Breaking Point: Being filled with the power of the
Holy Spirit

The Spirit can teach you just like He taught Elizabeth and showed her the gift that was in Mary. Search the Word of God to find out so much more concerning the Holy Spirit so you can better understand everything it means to be filled with His Spirit!

Remember the Holy Spirit is given as an outlet for the believer to plug into for power. The Holy Spirit is the power, and you are the vessel.

God is your provider; He never runs out, and He will fill you.

To be beautifully broken is to be empty of self and full of God.

Whenever you are feeling empty, tell yourself:

I AM BEAUTIFULLY FILLED!

Chapter Twelve

Beautifully Complete

With all of these chapters in place and active in your life, you should begin to feel completeness in your life. There is a wholeness that only comes from God. There is not a person or thing on earth that can complete you. A man does not complete you. Riches do not complete you. Family does not complete you. Friends do not complete you. Jesus Christ is the only one that completes you.

Colossians 2:9-10 "For in Him all the fullness of Deity dwells in bodily form, and in Him you have been made complete, and He is the head over all rule and authority."

If you have ever felt incomplete, there is hope. The feeling of being incomplete comes from the absence of the Lord. You determine how complete you will let God make you. Jesus was given to bring everything into fulfillment. He fulfilled the law and fulfilled the promises that we need to be complete. Anywhere there is an incomplete area; there is a need to let go and let God. Maybe you have not truly given every area to Him. You know you should, but it is hard for you to let go. Know that you can trust the Lord to complete you. You can trust that, if you give it to Him, He will make you whole again. You do not have to be afraid of letting go.

Philippians 1:6 "And I am sure of this, that he who began a good work in you will bring it to completion at the day of Jesus Christ."

God will complete what He started in you if you let Him. There's nothing lacking, nothing insecure, and nothing undone when you are in Christ. Everything you need to complete your purpose is found in Him. Everything you need for your future is found in Him. Everything you need to complete yourself is found in Him.

James 1:4 "Let perseverance finish its work so that you may be mature and complete, not lacking anything."

To be complete, you are going to have to persevere. Determine in your heart that, no matter what, you will stay in this race and fight for your faith. Know that there will be a day when you are physically, mentally, and spiritually complete all at once.

1 Corinthians 1:8 "He will also keep you firm to the end, so that you will be blameless on the day of our Lord Jesus Christ."

1 Thessalonians 5:23 "Now may the God of peace Himself sanctify you entirely; and may your spirit and soul and body be preserved complete, without blame at the coming of our Lord Jesus Christ."

God wants you not only complete in the time to come but also for today. The building is not the church; the people in the building are the church. You are the church.

Ephesians 1:23 "And the church is his body; it is made full and complete by Christ, who fills all things everywhere with himself."

Jesus can come into your life and fit Himself perfectly in it to make everything complete. He can complete every broken circumstance and every broken situation and bring it into line with His Word. You just have to obey His Word.

1 John 2:5 "But if anyone obeys his word, love for God is truly made complete in them."

Obedience to the Word of God brings completion. When you rely, hope, and trust in the Lord, every shattered piece in your life will be mended together to make you complete again. Everything you thought was lost, everything that you thought broke you, will become your testimony to all man. Humanity is not your enemy, it is your gift. What you had to go through in this life is a chance for God to make you complete. Being made complete in Christ is a platform to witness to all who are lost. Understanding that what you have gone through and what the Lord has done for you can help those around you to be complete too.

A testimony is twofold.

1) It is for you: to remind you of how far God has brought you and how much you have grown in Him.

2) It is for others: To declare how good God is to those who believe and to show them God can do the same in their lives.

I truly believe part of being complete is by sharing your testimony. I believe the Word when it says you overcome by the Blood of the Lamb and the word of your testimony. Your testimony matters. So I wanted to share mine with you. I am a work in progress. My prayer is that, through my personal testimony of how God made me complete, you will be blessed and open up your heart to being complete too.

My Personal Testimony:

My journey to being complete is not over yet. I have much learning and growth before me. What I have learned is to let God use me even if that might humiliate my flesh. Humility is a good thing, right? I grew up in church and knew the Word of God for the most part but still had quite the adventure in my walk with God growing up. When I was little, I loved God with all of my heart, but when I grew older, I departed from my faith. I thought I could live any way I wanted to and still be saved, but now I know that was not true. Here is how I made my way to being complete in Christ…

My journey to being Beautifully Loved:

I knew the love of a mother and a father, but I still searched for a love that was missing. I thought I could find it in a man, but I was very wrong. I thought people's love would satisfy me. I thought what they had to give is what I needed. I went from relationship to relationship just to end up with a broken heart. They said they loved me but it didn't last. I needed to find a love that lasted. I needed to find a love that could find me when I was lost and hold me when I was scared. It wasn't until I rededicated my life to Christ as a teenager that I found that love.

I realized the depth of God's love for me. I realized that His love is really all I needed. Once I received His love, I could truly love. Because I know the love of my Heavenly Father, I can now understand how to receive love and how to show love. God blessed me with a wonderful husband and two beautiful children to love. Now my favorite subject is His love. I know that I can't make it without it. My ultimate goal in life is to love like Christ loved. I want with all my heart to do everything in love! I praise God that He completes me with His love.

My journey to being Beautifully Forgiven:

I struggled very hard over this one. I have a past riddled with mistakes. I knew God's Word but in no way followed it. I discovered myself to be a hypocrite in what I did and said. I gave in to the temptations of lust and impurity and didn't know why God would forgive me if I knew better, but He did. One day I just gave my past to God and, all of the sudden I could feel the weight of my sin lifted off my conscience. When I prayed, I asked God to remove those sins from me as far as the east is from the west and He did! He took away the guilt and shame of who I used to be and what I used to do. He made me new. He showed me the error of my ways without condemning me. He allowed me to forgive myself for sinning against Him. Not once has He ever thrown anything in my face from my past. What is under the Blood is forgotten by Him. I thank Him for completing my forgiveness.

My journey to being Beautifully Created:

Where do I begin with this one? I went from being prideful in one moment to insecure in the next. At times I was arrogant and other times I had the lowest self-esteem ever. It is a funny thing to have to remind yourself pride comes before the fall and then other times have to remind yourself you are God's masterpiece. Being a woman is such a roller coaster. Before I had children, I was not insecure about my appearance. But when I had children, something happened. I was confident as a mother but broken as a person. I let the superficial take hold of the spiritual. I allowed the stretch marks that covered my body, and my outward appearance hurt my spirit. It's crazy how I let something so shallow affect me so deeply. I had to learn I am not this body; I am more than this flesh. I am the created of the Lord. I am His masterpiece, stretch marks and all. I may not look like the women in the magazines, but I am still beautifully created. I definitely had to let God humble me, and He became my confidence. I am confident in Him, not my flesh! He completes my confidence.

My journey to being Beautifully Destined:

I never in a million years thought God would use me like He has chosen to use me. I never thought I was good enough to be used greatly in His Kingdom. I always admired how God used others but never really saw Him using me like that. I would always doubt my purpose, partly because I didn't fully understand how He could use me and partly because I didn't think I had anything to offer. God showed me that everyone has something to offer. Everyone has a gift to give Him. I just had to learn to search the depths of my heart to see His plan for my life. And wouldn't you know it; He chose my greatest fear to be my purpose. He told me to step outside my comfort zone and speak. He told me to put myself out there to be used. I didn't like putting myself out there. Public speaking debilitated me. I trembled, I stuttered, and I fumbled over the easiest of words, but do you know what else? I survived. He saw me through to my purpose. There is no way I could do this without Him. I am nothing without Christ! He gave me something to say. He made up for my lack of ability and used me according to His plan. He helps me complete my destiny!

My journey to being Beautifully Free:

There are still days where I have to fight the good fight of faith for my freedom. I constantly struggled with fear and still have to overcome it by His Word every day. I would be afraid of the news and the way that the world is today. Every time I fear, I remember Jesus is stronger, and my fears are relieved. I had to believe God more than I believed my fears. I have struggled with addictions from which God taught me how to be free. God has freed me from the opinions of man and the stereotypes that have been placed on me by the culture in which we live. I used to think that I had to be everything that others expected me to be but God freed me when He reminded me I only have to be who He has called me to be. I had to fill the shoes that He set before me and no one else's. Thank You, Lord, for completing my freedom!

My journey to being Beautifully Healed:

I have needed healing in all areas of my life. I have needed healing in my body, mind, and spirit. When I was born, I had a club foot. They said I would have to always wear special leg braces, but the Lord healed me in my body! Not only did I not need the leg braces but He completely straightened out my leg. I can run and jump and do everything I need to do. Praise God! I have let my mind be full of negative thoughts and feelings, but the Lord replaced them all with the mind of Christ and healed my mind. He now regulates my thoughts and leaves no room for depression. When I was offended in the church, or hurt by fellow believers, He healed my crushed spirit. He is my Healer! By His stripes, I am healed! Thank You, Lord, for making my mind, body, and spirit completely whole!

My journey to being Beautifully Happy:

I have had dark clouds that have tried to stick around my life. Whether brought on by current circumstances, or my own doing, God taught me to be happy through the darkness of the clouds. He taught me that brighter days are ahead and gave me permission to be happy in Him. I know what it is like to be unhappy, and I know what it is like to be happy. Happiness is always better than unhappiness, so I had to learn to choose happiness. I had to learn that my happiness could not come from things of this world but through the things of God. God gave me joy to be my strength when I am weak, so I am going to hang on to it no matter what. I have learned to smile and appreciate every day. Be happy in every day because you never know when your last day will be. Thank You, Lord, for making my joy complete!

My journey to being Beautifully Different:

Most people do not want to be different; for the most part, they want to fit in, and I wanted to fit in. I wanted to fit in with the clothes I wore and the way I looked. I wanted to do what everyone else did and act like they acted. Praise God, He showed me a better way. He showed me that my life would be better when I was different. He transformed me from the inside out. I do not have to struggle like the world anymore because He taught me how to be different. I do not have to fit in, I have to stand out. He taught me to stand when everyone else bowed, to bow when everyone else stood, and to speak when everyone else was silent. The Lord taught me that I was not missing out on anything by being different. I was actually gaining blessing by being different than everyone else. It is because I changed the way I lived after I got saved that I am blessed. I could not have stayed in the race without the transformation

Christ made in me. The new way God has is so much better than the old way. Thank You, Lord, for making me complete by making me different.

My journey to being Beautifully Approved:

I have always cared about other people's approval. I was and am a people pleaser. I understand that being a people pleaser is not bad, but I had to learn to please God first. I had to grow in the knowledge that getting God's approval is the most important approval that I could ever receive. I had to learn to please God even if that meant disappointing people. By pleasing God, I was not only approved by God, but I was also approved by the right people. I learned it is okay to have the approval of others as long as it never interfered with the approval of God. Being a chameleon in situations just to please the people I was around taught me the dangers of trying to please everyone. I will be respectful and kind, but I won't change who I am in God just so I can be approved by man. I need God's consent and approval in everything I do to keep me from destruction. I thank the Lord for sending Jesus so that I could be completely approved.

My journey to being Beautifully Wise:

I still have a long, long, long way to go on this one. I definitely do not know all that I could, but I am striving toward the mark by learning more of His Word. I struggle with memorization every now and then (honestly, I struggle with it more often than not) so I really have to focus on retaining in my heart all that I read in the Word. I know that my wisdom comes from the Lord and if I seek Him, I will find Him. I have to make time to get into His Word for my wisdom because if I do not, my flesh will have its way and be lazy and not wise. I have learned to take lessons from other people and pray that I will always be teachable in His Word. I do not always like to be corrected, but wisdom tells me I often need to be. I know if I stay in His Word and apply His Word, I will be blessed. Thank You, Lord, for helping make me complete in your wisdom.

My journey to being Beautifully Filled:

I wrote earlier about my fear so you know I had to learn to let God fill me with peace. There would be nights that I would toss and turn; I would beg for God to fill me with peace and that is when I realized that my peace relied on how much I trusted God. He could only fill me with peace when I trusted Him. I am a clinger. I liked to hold on to things, but God taught me to let go. He taught me that I had to empty myself of what I clung to so that He could fill me with what I needed. He filled me with hope and made me realize there is hope in every situation if I would just let Him take care of it. He gave me the comfort of the Holy Spirit when I stopped questioning His Word concerning it. I had to trust God's Word about the Spirit and not doubt it. Thank You, Lord, for making me complete by filling me up!

I am not all that I want to be yet, but I am, for sure, not who I used to be. I am still running this race, praying that I will let God make me beautifully broken all along the way.

I sincerely hope that I revealed my heart to you in a way that you will be encouraged to let the Lord make you beautifully broken too. It will be quite the adventure seeing every broken piece of our lives put back together by God in the most beautiful of ways. Our ashes for His beauty and our hearts in His hands make us beautifully broken!

To be beautifully broken is to be complete in Christ.

You are beautifully complete in Christ!

Anytime you are lacking, and anytime you feel incomplete, tell yourself:

I AM BEAUTIFULLY COMPLETE!

Thank you so much for taking the time to read Beautifully Broken. I hope you know that you are greatly loved by God!

CONNECT
Twitter @mandyfender11
Facebook Mandy Fender Author Page
http://mandyfender.com/